First World War
and Army of Occupation
War Diary
France, Belgium and Germany

51 DIVISION
152 Infantry Brigade,
Brigade Trench Mortar Battery
1 August 1916 - 31 August 1916

WO95/2868/4

The Naval & Military Press Ltd
www.nmarchive.com
Published in association with The National Archives

Published by

The Naval & Military Press Ltd

Unit 10 Ridgewood Industrial Park,

Uckfield, East Sussex,

TN22 5QE England

Tel: +44 (0) 1825 749494

www.naval-military-press.com

www.nmarchive.com

This diary has been reprinted in facsimile from the original. Any imperfections are inevitably reproduced and the quality may fall short of modern type and cartographic standards.

© Crown Copyright
Images reproduced by permission of The National Archives, London, England, 2015.

Contents

Document type	Place/Title	Date From	Date To
Heading	WO95/2868 Brigade Trench Mortar Battery Aug 1916		
Heading	51st Division 152nd Infy Bde 152nd Trench Mortar Bty. Aug 1916		
Heading	War Diary Of 152nd Trench Mortar Battery August 1916 Vol 1		
War Diary		01/08/1916	31/08/1916
Miscellaneous	Herewith Enclosed War Diary For The Month Of August	05/09/1916	05/09/1916
Miscellaneous	On October 11th 1918 the Battery moved	01/11/1918	01/11/1918

(4)

WO95/2868

Brigade Trench Mortar Battery

Aug 1916

51ST DIVISION
152ND INFY BDE

152ND TRENCH MORTAR BTY
AUG 1916

WAR DIARY
of
152nd Trench Mortar Battery.

AUGUST, 1916.

WAR DIARY or **INTELLIGENCE=SUMMARY**

Army Form C. 2118.

CONFIDENTIAL

1st Huts No 21(A) 7 HIGHLAND DIVISION

(Erase heading not required.)

Instructions regarding War Diaries and Intelligence Summaries are contained in F. S. Regs., Part II. and the Staff Manual respectively. Title Pages will be prepared in manuscript.

Place	Date	Hour	Summary of Events and Information	Remarks and references to Appendices
Tuesday	1st Aug.	-	Reconnoitred High Wood for gun positions. Gun positions improved.	
Wednesday	2nd "	"	Gun positions improved.	
Thursday	3rd "	"	280 rounds fired by 4 guns. Guns engaged in reaching S.W. corner of High Wood to 400 yards N.E.	
Friday	4th "	"	Improving gun positions. Pte Land wounded.	
Saturday	5th "	"	In trenches at HIGH WOOD. Pte Pratt wounded. At 6.2 a.m. 4 guns fired 290 rounds; 4 of these being laid on German strong point to RIGHT of HIGH WOOD, the remainder reaching the S.W. corner of WOOD. The enemy's artillery retaliated for over half an hour.	
Sunday	6th "	"	Trenches at HIGH WOOD. Work done on gun positions.	
Monday	7th "	"	Relieved in HIGH WOOD by 100th T.M.B. at 6 a.m. marched to DERNANCOURT when the battery bivouacked.	
Tuesday	8th "	"	Rested at DERNANCOURT.	
Wednesday	9th "	"	Marched to MERICOURT and entrained for LONGPRÉ.	

Army Form C. 2118.

WAR DIARY
or
INTELLIGENCE SUMMARY
(Erase heading not required.)

Instructions regarding War Diaries and Intelligence Summaries are contained in F. S. Regs., Part II. and the Staff Manual respectively. Title Pages will be prepared in manuscript.

Place	Date	Hour	Summary of Events and Information	Remarks and references to Appendices
Thursday	10	Aug	Billeted in LONGPRE	Reference M.H.P
Friday	11	"	Two officers & 12 men reported for duty with battery. Entrained in the early evening at LONGPRE for THIENNES.	HAZEBROUCK 5.A Scale 1/100,000
Saturday	12	"	Arrived at THIENNES early in the morning. Marched to billets in BARINGHEM.	
Sunday	13	"	En. rd billets at BLARINGHEM. Captain Amos to hospital (sick) on 15th	
Monday	14	"	Two classes of instruction in Stokes Gun completed.	
Tuesday	15	"		
Wednesday	16	"		
Thursday	17	"	The Brigadier General inspected the battery and was highly pleased with the appearance and the turn-out of the men. In the evening the 7 guns and all tools were handed over to O.C. No 2 N.Z. T.M.B.	
Friday	18	"	Entrained from ERQUINGHEM in the afternoon to STEENWERCK. Entrained from there to billets in ARMENTIÈRES.	
Saturday	19	"	Took over guns, tools & stores from the 2nd N.Z. T.M.B. 3rd course of instruction started	
Sunday	20	"	Two officers came to battery for instruction & duty (temporary).	

Army Form C. 2118.

WAR DIARY
INTELLIGENCE SUMMARY
(Erase heading not required.)

Instructions regarding War Diaries and Intelligence Summaries are contained in F. S. Regs., Part II. and the Staff Manual respectively. Title Pages will be prepared in manuscript.

Place	Date	Hour	Summary of Events and Information	Remarks and references to Appendices
Monday	21st Aug	—	One officer & two N.C.O's went to TERDEGHEM for instruction in Stokes gun.	
Tuesday	22nd "	"	Still in billets at ARMENTIERES.	MAP REFERENCE
Wednesday	23rd "	"		HAZEBROUCK
Thursday	24th "	"	9 men joined for duty on 22nd "	S^A Scale 1/100,000
Friday 25th	25th "	—	Inspected by the Brigadier-General in goo-tilined drill. Battery churned in "shorts"; blue flannies & shirt puttees. Also wearing tam-o-shanties.	
Saturday 26th	26th "	"	Relieved the 152nd T.M.B. in the trenches. Guns etc were carried up & the relief completed by 11.50 a.m. Orders were received at 8.15 from gpo obj., some new positions had to be prepared as some of the positions taken over, were not in gaps. Left time about 11.30 pm. Reference map for operations in new positions now moved 36 N W 4
Sunday	29th "	—	126 rounds fired. One gun out of action owing to strikes taking faulty. The enemy's trenches were engaged at seven points. The majority of shots landed with good effect. Planks, picks, bags, etc were seen blown up. The rounds were fired at the same time. The enemy retaliated with heavy trench mortars & "whizz-bangs" causing little damage. The gun positions were improved during the day.	9 Hopkins 36 NW NE 4
Tuesday	28th "	"	116 rounds fired by the nine guns. Most of the day was devoted to ranging. Only two guns (on the left) drew retaliation from heavy mortars. Most of the shots was small damage. The ranging was very difficult owing to the wind. Being rainy. The base plate of 9 legs slipped every time the gun was fired. Although there was a layer of brick, forming a foundation to the base plate, it was proved not to be sufficient	E (Oct) Sketch 13 Map 1/10,000

Army Form C. 2118.

WAR DIARY
INTELLIGENCE SUMMARY
(Erase heading not required.)

Instructions regarding War Diaries and Intelligence Summaries are contained in F. S. Regs., Part II. and the Staff Manual respectively. Title Pages will be prepared in manuscript.

Place	Date	Hour	Summary of Events and Information	Remarks and references to Appendices
Tuesday	29" Aug		45 rounds were fired in registration. The day was very rainy. Busy in preparing belts for the Browning-Hotchkiss. Very difficult work owing to weather & the nature of ground. Two guns from the 134th M.M.G. came up in the night.	
Wednesday	30" Aug		149 rounds were fired by eight guns. There were fired at 9.57 p.m. Great difficulty was again experienced with the sinking of the Browning-Hotchkiss. Owing to this these guns were temporally put out of action, whenever a hole was dug in, filled up, almost at once, with water. The enemy retaliated with eight shells and machine gun fire. A very windy day.	
Thursday	31" Aug		701 rounds were fired during intense artillery bombardment at 1.30 p.m. on enemy's front line trenches along the watch-dog front. Retaliation for this bombardment was not very effective. Position of T.M. Rds fired Targets Engaged. T 5.c.6.7 — 80 T 5.a.c.7.8 — 92 — T 5.d.4.6, T 5.d.5.5 T 5.a.7.4 — 100 — T 5.b.6, T 5.d.4.3 T 10.B.9.4 — 50 — T 11.a.6.5 T 11.A.3.6 — 76 — T 11.a.6.0 T 11.c.2.7 — 50 — T 11.c.6.7 T 10.d.6.1 — 58 — T 17.a.4.7 T 10.d.7.2 — 97 — T 17.a.3.6 T 10.D.8.4 — 72 — T 11.b.7.0, T 11.c.7.6.2	See 152 hy/Bde Operation order No. 61.

To 152 Inf Brigade Headquarters
From O.C. 152 Trench Mortar Battery

Herewith enclosed War Diary for the month of August.

Thomas F. Harvey 2/Lt
for O.C. 152 T.M.B.

5-9-16

152nd TRENCH MORTAR BATTERY

On October 11th 1918 the Battery moved from Bourlon Wood to Escaudoeuvres where they remained for the night.

On the morning of 12th October 1918 an officer and 30 O.R.s went into the line with 3 guns & were attached to 5th Seaforth Highlanders coming under orders of the C.O. of this Battalion.

During the attack on the morning of 12th October 1918 the Battery moved forward with three guns with the right support company of the right Battalion, as far as the village of Avesnes-le-Sec where the officer made his H.Q.

A message was sent by the Battery Officer to O.C. right company informing him of his H.Q. so that guns could be sent forward if required.

The guns were not called upon as no target within range presented itself.

The Battery remained in the village of Avesnes-le-Sec for the night of 12th Oct.

On the morning of 13th October 1918 orders were received from C.O. 5th Seaforth Highlanders to move forward with guns along with C Coy of 5th Seaforth Highlanders (second wave)

Strong artillery fire & M.G. fire was met with as soon as they moved forward.

Many of the ammunition carrying party became casualties as soon as they moved from the jumping off line. The remainder went forward under 2/Lieut. J Bruce 5th Seaforth Highlanders attached to this Battery, with the second wave.

Two guns were brought into action at O.15.b. firing on hostile M.G. in ruined house at cross-roads in O.10.c.

After firing several rounds the gun teams became casualties & had to withdraw, 240848 Cpl. Mayoh S. of 5th Seaforth Highlanders continuing to fire alone until he himself became a casualty.

By this time practically all the personnel had become casualties. The remainder became attached to a party of 6th Gordon Highlanders as infantry, and remainded with them until the night of the 14th October 1918.

The Officer was also attached to the 5th Seaforth Highlanders as an infantry officer until ordered to return to Battery H.Q. with the men he had with him, under Brigade orders.

Since this date the Battery has not been in action, but has supplied 2 or 3 working parties & carried out salvaging while at Iwuy.

1/11/18.

H Blackstock Capt.
Condg 152 T M B